WHAT IF THERE WERE NO BEES?

A Book about the Grassland Ecosystem

by Suzanne Slade

illustrated by Carol Schwartz

PICTURE WINDOW BOOKS
a capstone imprint

DON'T BE FOOLED BY A BEE'S SIZE. It's tiny compared to the foxes, skunks, and owls that share its grassland home. But bees do the work of giants! Bees spend countless hours darting from flower to flower to collect pollen and nectar.

GRASSLAND PLANTS, ANIMALS, AND INSECTS are tied to one another by food chains. Bees, as well as other living things, belong to several chains. Many food chains are connected by one plant or animal to create larger food webs.

FOX

BIRD

MOUSE

BEAR

SPIDER

HONEY

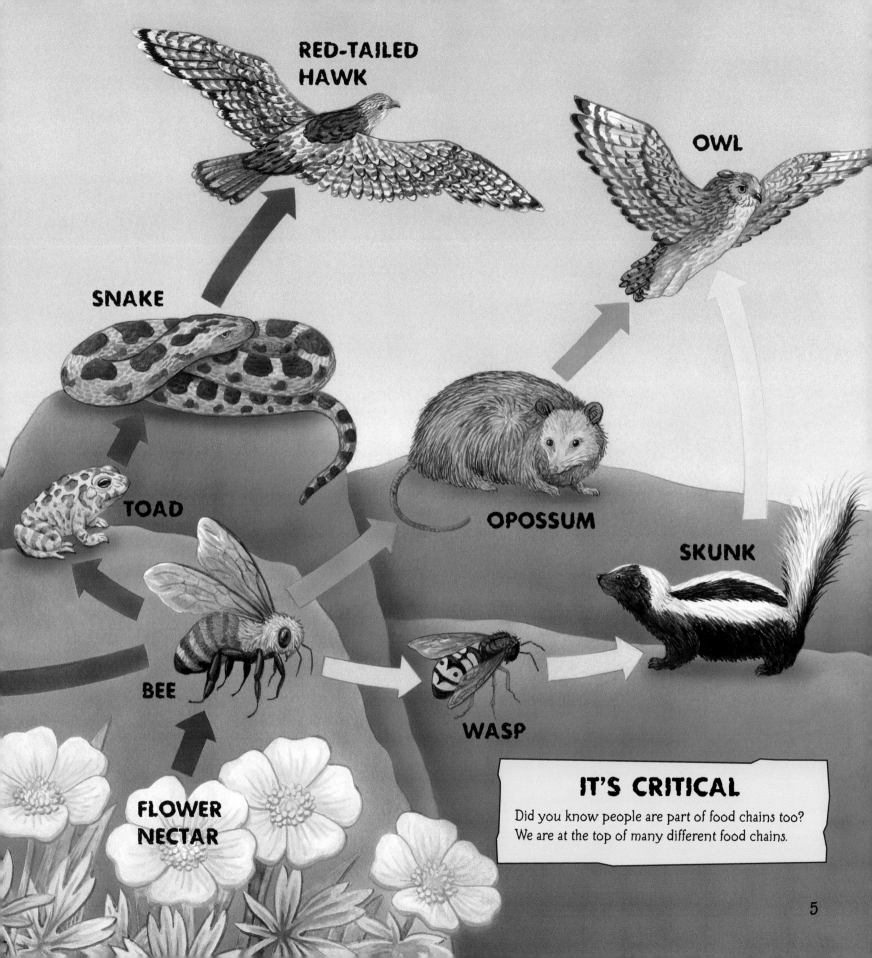

RED-TAILED HAWK

OWL

SNAKE

TOAD

OPOSSUM

SKUNK

BEE

WASP

FLOWER NECTAR

IT'S CRITICAL

Did you know people are part of food chains too? We are at the top of many different food chains.

5

FLOWERS ARE A BEE'S BEST FRIEND. They're often filled with a sweet liquid called nectar. Bees sip nectar to keep up their energy. Honey bees also use nectar to make honey.

As bees collect nectar, tiny pieces of pollen stick to their furry legs. When bees visit other flowers, the pollen falls off. Flowering plants need pollen to create seeds and fruits. This process is called pollination.

IT'S CRITICAL

Bees usually stay within 2 miles (3.2 kilometers) of their hive. If they can't find enough nectar, some bees will travel up to 7 miles (11.3 km) from home.

AS BEES FLY AROUND to collect food, they face many dangers. Spiders, birds, toads, and other hungry predators hunt these hardworking insects. Pollution and some of the pesticides farmers use to protect their crops can also hurt bees.

IT'S CRITICAL

Since 2006, more and more honey bee colonies are dying unexpectedly. Worried beekeepers aren't sure why so many colonies are disappearing. Some people believe bee diseases, pesticides, poor eating, and stress are harming bee health.

Mice often make unwelcome nests in honey bee boxes. While the mice aren't dangerous to the bees, they do damage the boxes and the bees' honeycomb. The smell of mouse droppings may cause bees to leave their hive for good.

WHAT WOULD HAPPEN IF BEES BECAME EXTINCT?

If there were no bees, farmers near grasslands would have a lot of trouble growing crops. Farmers need bees, especially honey bees, to help pollinate their fruit and nut trees. Apple, cherry, plum, and avocado trees would produce less fruit—or none at all—without bees. Almond and macadamia trees would produce less too.

IT'S CRITICAL

Sometimes a plant or animal species is so important that without it many other species could become extinct. It's called a keystone species. Bees are a keystone species. Keystone species help make sure an ecosystem has many types of life in it.

11

FIELDS OF STRAWBERRY PLANTS wouldn't be able to produce fruit. Neither would blueberry plants. Without bees, there would be fewer carrots, onions, and other vegetables. Bees are major pollinators of many fruit and vegetable crops.

IT'S CRITICAL

Honey bees pollinate about 90 different crops in North America. They help create about one-third of the food we eat. Some farmers hire beekeepers to bring hives of bees to pollinate their fields. The bees stay a few weeks, then they are moved to another field.

GRASSLAND WILDFLOWERS and other plants couldn't make seeds without bees. Flowering bushes in nearby forests couldn't grow berries for birds. Soon, many mice, squirrels, and other small animals would not have enough food to survive.

IT'S CRITICAL

With fewer small animals, larger animals would be in trouble too. Foxes, owls, and other meat-eaters would have a tougher time finding food.

15

IT'S CRITICAL

About one-fifth of a black bear's diet comes from honey, plus the fruits, nuts, and berries pollinated by bees. Without bees, black bears would be forced to move to new areas in search of food.

HONEY BEES MAKE HONEY from the nectar they collect. Bears, skunks, mice, and ants love the sweet honey. It's an important food source for them. Without honey, these animals, and many others, would suffer.

WITHOUT BEES, grasslands and nearby farms and forests would become quieter, less colorful places.

FEWER TRUCKLOADS OF FRESH FRUITS AND VEGETABLES.

NO FLOWERING PLANTS BLANKETING THE WIDE, OPEN FIELDS.

NO BRIGHT BERRIES OR CRUNCHY SEEDS FOR THE FOREST ANIMALS TO EAT.

What would happen if bees became extinct? **ALL KINDS OF THINGS!**

The loss of one small creature, even as small as the bee, can have a huge effect on the ecosystems of our world. Today scientists are studying bees closely to learn how to keep them safe and healthy. Farmers are finding new ways to control pests. All this hard work should mean more bees buzzing around in the future!

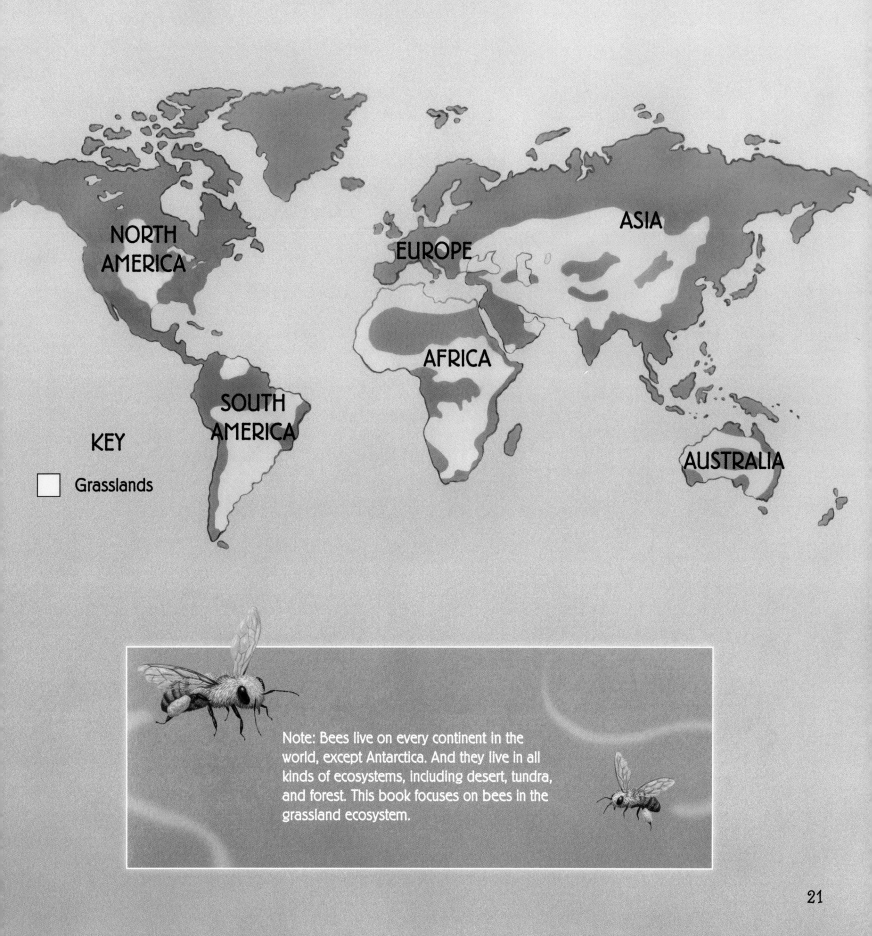

NORTH
AMERICA

EUROPE

ASIA

AFRICA

SOUTH
AMERICA

AUSTRALIA

KEY

Grasslands

Note: Bees live on every continent in the world, except Antarctica. And they live in all kinds of ecosystems, including desert, tundra, and forest. This book focuses on bees in the grassland ecosystem.

GRASSLAND ANIMALS IN DANGER

The following animal populations are in danger of becoming extinct if nothing is done to protect them:

masked bobwhite

Utah prairie dog

prairie chicken

masked bobwhite

HOW TO HELP KEEP OUR GRASSLANDS HEALTHY

• Make your yard more beautiful and provide nectar for bees at the same time by planting flowers.

• Be a part of National Pollinator Week the last week of June. Search for "National Pollinator Week" online to learn how you can celebrate and help bees, butterflies, and other pollinators.

• If you find a beehive or a wild bee colony, walk away slowly and leave it alone. Bees have an important job to do. They work best if they are not disturbed.

• Find natural ways to get rid of pesky bugs in your yard. By using fewer pesticides, which can harm bees and other helpful insects, you're helping all the animals around you.

Glossary

colony–a group whose members live and work together

ecosystem–a group of plants and animals living together, along with the place where they live

extinct–no longer living anywhere on Earth

food chain–a group of living things that are connected because each one eats the other

food web–many food chains connected together

nectar–a sweet liquid formed inside flowers

pesticide–a chemical used to kill harmful pests

pollen–a powder formed inside flowers

pollination–the act of spreading pollen from one plant to another so the plant is able to make more plants

predator–an animal that hunts other animals for food

species–a group of plants or animals that has many things in common

To Learn More

More Books to Read

Mortensen, Lori. *In the Trees, Honey Bees.* Sharing Nature with Children Book. Nevada City, Calif.: Dawn Publications, 2009.

Rockwell, Anne. *Honey in a Hive.* Let's-Read-and-Find-Out Science. New York: HarperCollins, 2005.

Slade, Suzanne. *What Do You Know About Food Chains and Food Webs?* 20 Questions: Science. New York: PowerKids Press, 2008.

Internet Sites

FactHound offers a safe, fun way to find Internet sites related to this book.
All of the sites on FactHound have been researched by our staff.

Here's all you do:
Visit *www.facthound.com*
Type in this code: 9781404860193

Index

Look for all the books in the Food Chain Reactions series:

What If There Were No Bees? A Book about the Grassland Ecosystem

What If There Were No Gray Wolves? A Book about the Temperate Forest Ecosystem

What If There Were No Lemmings? A Book about the Tundra Ecosystem

What If There Were No Sea Otters? A Book about the Ocean Ecosystem

Special thanks to our advisers for their expertise:
Erin W. Hodgson, PhD, Extension Entomologist
Iowa State University, Ames, Iowa

Terry Flaherty, PhD, Professor of English
Minnesota State University, Mankato

Picture Window Books
1710 Roe Crest Drive
North Mankato, MN 56003
www.capstonepub.com

Editor: Jill Kalz
Designer: Lori Bye
Art Director: Nathan Gassman
Production Specialist: Jane Klenk
The illustrations in this book were created with traditional illustration, gouache, airbrush, and digitally.

Library of Congress Cataloging-in-Publication Data
Slade, Suzanne.
  What if there were no bees? : a book about the grassland ecosystem / by Suzanne Slade ; illustrated by Carol Schwartz.
    p. cm. — (Food chain reactions)
  Includes index.
  ISBN 978-1-4048-6019-3 (library binding)
  ISBN 978-1-4048-6394-1 (paperback)
  1. Bees—Control—Environmental aspects—United States—Juvenile literature. 2. Bees—Control—Environmental aspects—United States. 3. Pollination by insects—Juvenile literature. 4. Pollination by insects. 5. Agricultural ecology—United States—Juvenile literature. 6. Agricultural ecology—United States. I. Schwartz, Carol, 1954– ill. II. Title.
  QK926.S53 2011
  577.4—dc22
                              2010006035

Printed in the United States   5957